Table of Contents

Inside maps and flags have been left blank so that the students may color them when they have completed the song. Refer to the cover for the appropriate colors.

©1993 by Hi. I. Que Publishing, P.O. Box 508,
Claremont, California 91711 • (909) 622-7501
International copyright secured.
All rights reserved.
Printed in U.S.A.

ISBN 0-9631333-1-4

Hi. I Que Publishing
Claremont, California 91711

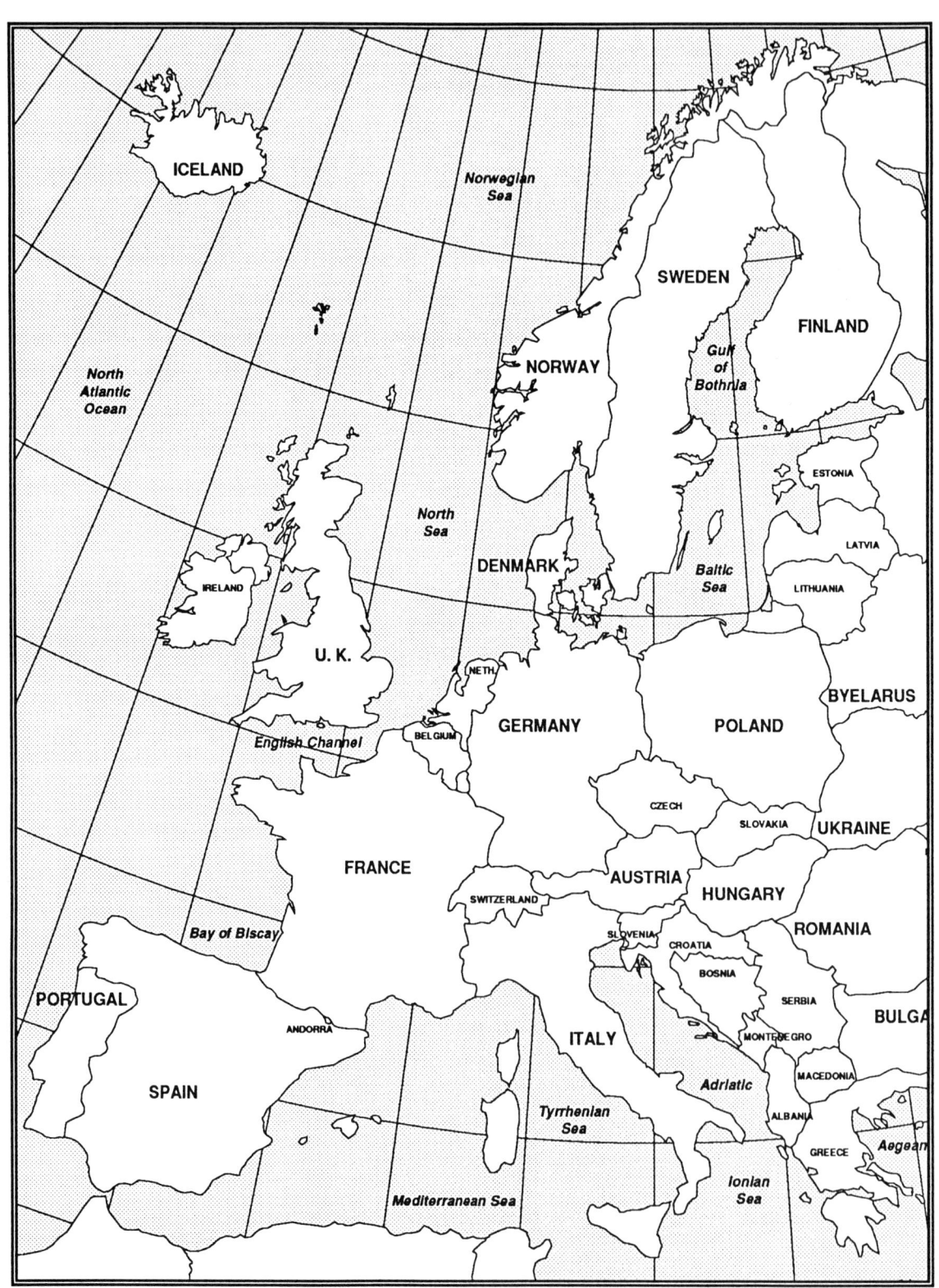

Introduction

The purpose of this anthology is to provide students with access to National Anthems throughout the world.

Each country introduces it's children to their National Anthem early in life. Schools, parents and government are usually all involved in instilling pride in a child toward his/her own country.

It should be understood by all, that while there may be differences toward governments and cultures, people are inherently equal worldwide. Each person should be able to have pride for the soil on which they were born. Each person should be able to learn respect for another persons pride in their country.

One step in accomplishing this goal, hopefully, is to introduce the student to the anthems of other countries.

Through listening to the anthems of another country and giving thought to the words included, it is hoped that each person will become aware and learn to respect the pride another individual has toward their country.

We hope this education will help promote peace and respect among all.

ANDORRA

Form of Government: *Principality*

Predominant Languages: *Catalan (Official), French, Spanish*

Capital: *Andorra*

Currency: *French franc, Spanish peseta*

National Holiday: *Mare de Dev de Meritxell, September 8th*

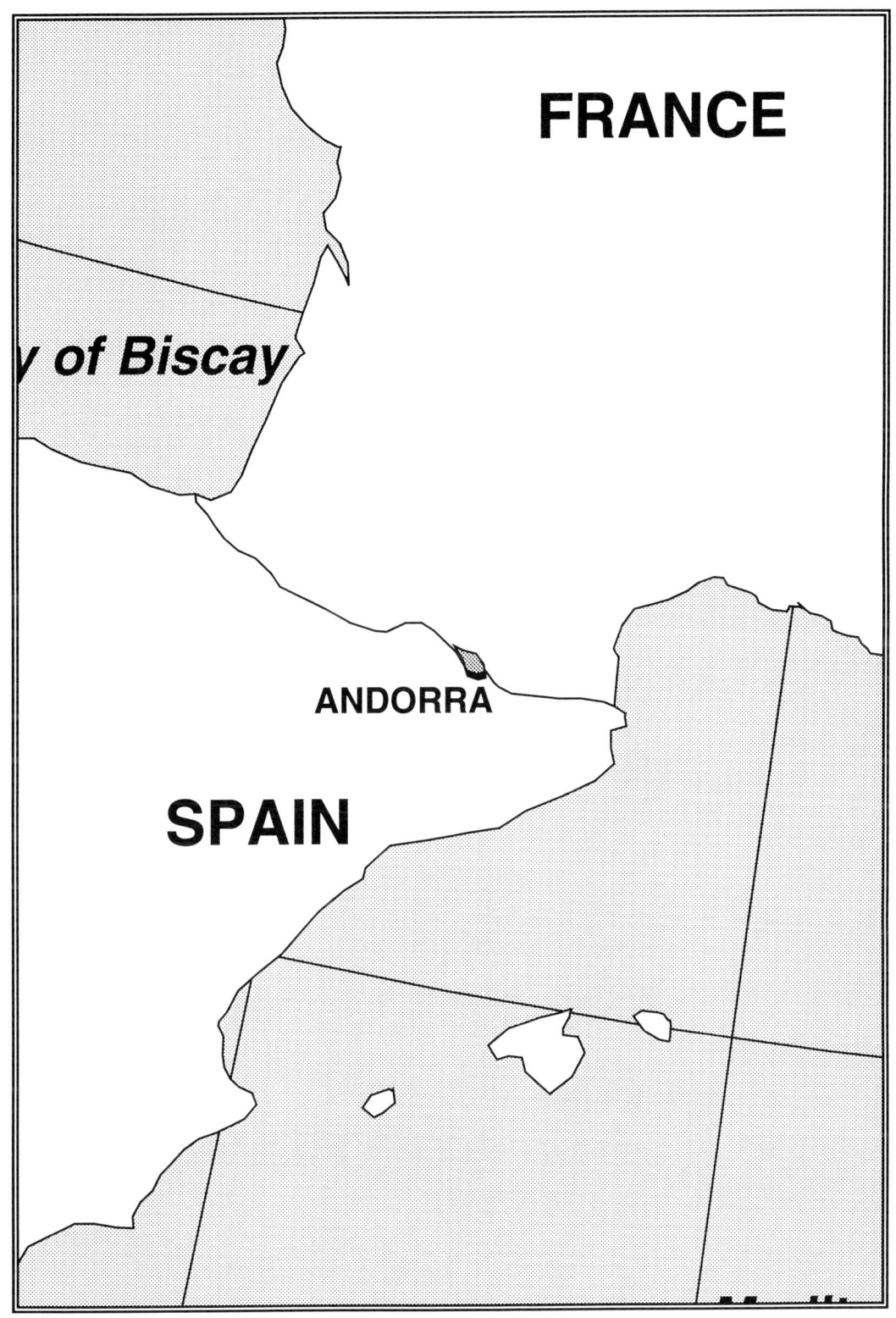

NATIONAL ANTHEM OF ANDORRA:

(CATALAN)

EL GRAN CARLEMANY, MON PARE,
DELS ALARBS ME DESLLIURA,
I DEL CEL VIDAEM DONA DE
MERITXELL LA GRAN MARE.
PRINCESA NAS QUII PUBILLA ENTRE
DOS NACIONS NEUTRAL;
SOLS RESTO LUNICA FILLA
DEL IMPERI CARLEMANY.
CREIENT I LLIURE ONSE SEGLES,
CREIENT I LLIURE VULL SER.
SIGUEN ELS FURS MOSTUTORS
I MOS PRINCEPS DEFENSORS!
I MOS PRINCEPS DEFENSORS!

NATIONAL ANTHEM OF ANDORRA:

(ENGLISH TRANSLATION)

THE GREAT CHARLEMAGNE, MY FATHER,
FREED ME FROM THE ARABS,
AND FROM HEAVEN HE GAVE ME LIFE OF
MERITXELL THE GREAT MOTHER.
I WAS BORN A PRINCESS NATION,
NEUTRAL BETWEEN TWO NATIONS;
I AM NOW THE ONLY DAUGHTER
OF THE CAROLINGIAN EMPIRE.
BELIEVING AND FREE FOR ELEVEN
CENTURIES,
BELIEVING AND FREE I WILL STAY.
OUR LAWS WILL BE MY TEACHERS
AND PRINCES WILL DEFEND ME!
AND PRINCES WILL DEFEND ME!

National Anthem of Andorra

Words by
The Hon. Dr. D. Joan Benlloch I Vivo (1864-1926)

Melody by
Father Enric Marfany (1871-1942)

BELGIUM

Form of Government: *Constitutional Monarchy*

Predominant Languages: *Dutch, French*

Capital: *Brussels*

Currency: *Franc*

National Holiday: *National Day, July 21st (ascension of King Leopold to the throne in 1831)*

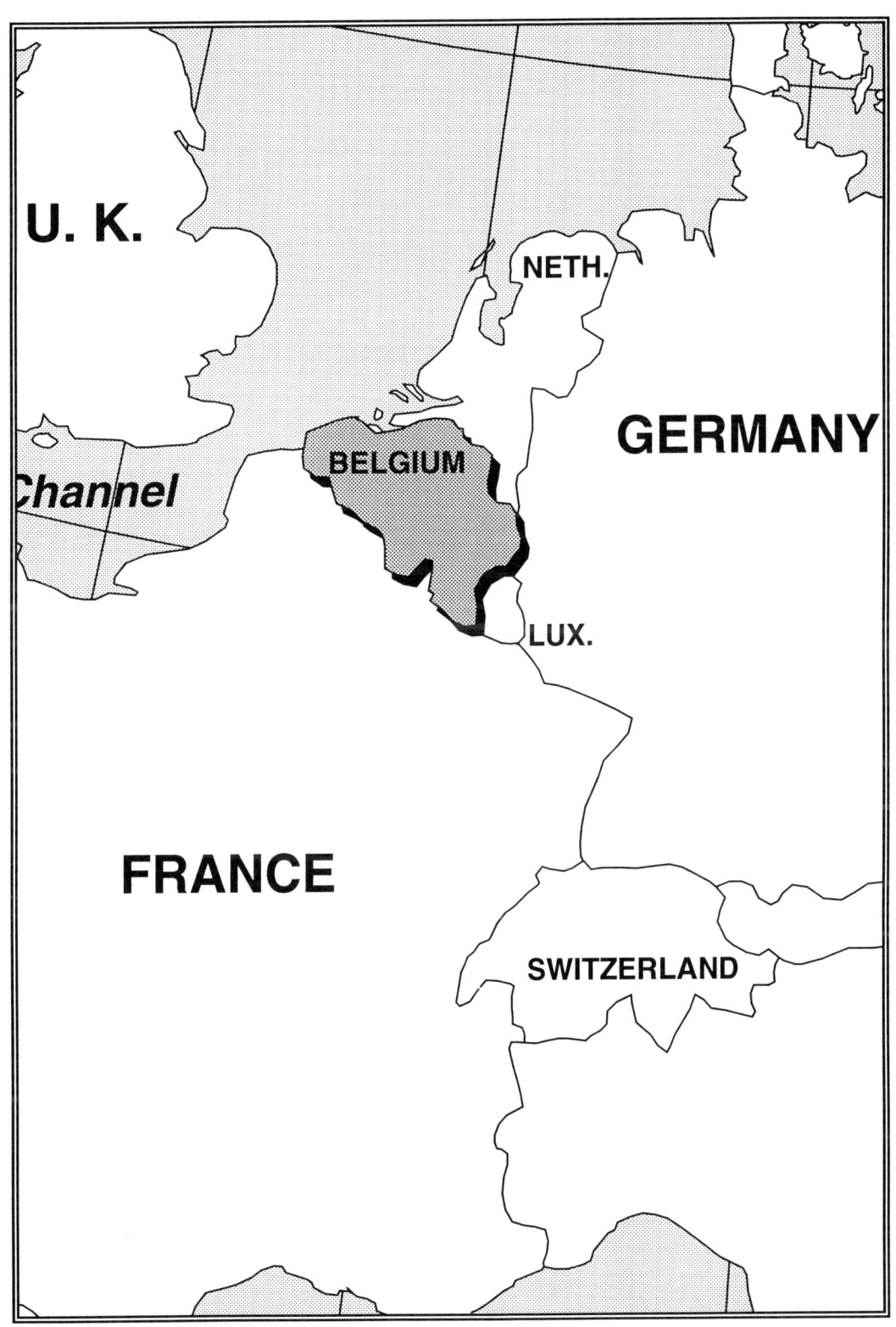

NATIONAL ANTHEM OF BELGIUM: LA BRABANCONNE

(FRENCH)

APRES DES SIECLES D'ESCLAVA GE,
LE BALGE, SORTANT DU TOMBEAU,
A RECONQUIS PAR SON CONRAGE SON NOM,
SES DROITS ET SON DRAPEAU.
ET TA MAIN SOUVERAINE ET FIERE,
PEUPLE DESORMAIS INDOMPTE,
GRAVA SUR TA VIEILLE BANNIERE:
LE ROI, LE LOI, LA LIBERTE,
GRAVA SUR TA VIEILLE BANNIERE:
LE ROI, LA LOI, LA LIBERTE,
LE ROI, LA LOI, LA LIBERTE,
LE ROI, LA LOI, LA LIBERTE.

(DUTCH)

O DIERBAAR BELGIE,
O HEILIG LAND DER VAADREN,
ONZE ZIEL EN ONS HART ZIJN U GEWIJD.
AANVAARD ONS KRACHT
EN HET BLOED VAN ONS AADREN,
WEES ONS DOEL IN ARBEID EN IN STRIJD.
BLOEI, O LAND, IN EENDRACHT NIET TE
BREKEN, WEES IMMER U ZELF EN ONGEKNECHT
HET WOORD GETROUW
DAT GE ONBEVREESD MOOGT SPREKEN,
VOOR VORST, VOOR VRIJHEID EN VOOR RECHT,
HET WOORD GETROUW
DAT GE ONBEVREESD MOOGT SPREKEN,
VOOR VORST, VOOR VRIJHEID EN VOOR RECHT,
VOOR VORST, VOOR VRIJHEID EN VOOR RECHT,
VOOR VORST, VOOR VRIJHEID EN VOOR RECHT.

NATIONAL ANTHEM OF BELGIUM:
LA BRABANCONNE

(ENGLISH TRANSLATION)

FROM THE DEPTHS OF BONDAGE AND
SLAVERY BELGIUM HAS FINALLY BEEN FREED;
AND HAS REGAINED THROUGH HER BRAVERY,
HER NAME, HER FLAG, HER FREEDOM;
AND BY APPEARANCE,
FEARLESS AND SUCCESSFULL SINCE THAT DAY,
UPHOLDING YOUR CAUSE,
IS BURNED ON YOUR ANCIENT
AND GLORIOUS FLAG,
YOUR KING, YOUR FREEDOM AND YOUR LAWS,
IS BURNED ON YOUR ANCIENT GLORIOUS
FLAG,
YOUR KING, YOUR FREEDOM AND YOUR LAWS,
YOUR KING, YOUR FREEDOM AND YOUR LAWS,
YOUR KING, YOUR FREEDOM AND YOUR LAWS.

National Anthem of Belgium

Words by
Charles Rogier (1800-1885)

Melody by
Francois Van Campenhout (1779-1848)

DENMARK

Form of Government: *Constitutional Monarchy*

Predominant Language: *Danish*

Capital: *Copenhagen*

Currency: *Krone*

National Holiday: *Birthday of the Queen, April 16th (1940)*

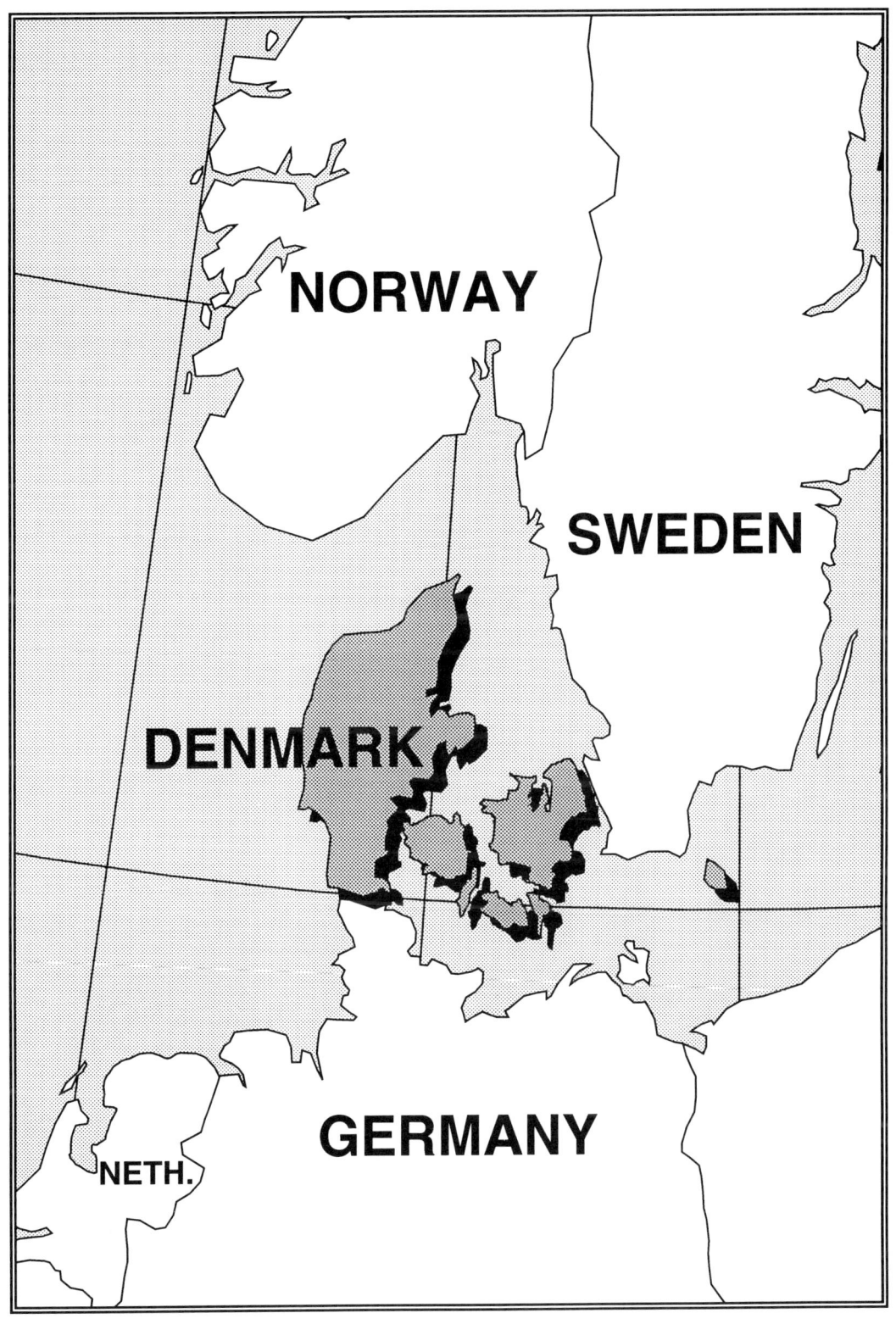

NATIONAL ANTHEM OF DENMARK:
KONG KRISTIAN
TO BE PLAYED ONLY IN THE PRESENCE OF DANISH ROYALTY.

(DANISH)

KONG KRISTIAN STOD VED HOJEN MAST
I ROG OG DAMP.
HANS VOERGE HAMREDE SA FAST,
AT GOTENS HJOELM OG HJERNE BRAST;
DA SANK HVER FJENDTLIGT SPEJL OG
MAST
I ROG OG DAMP.
"FLY", SKREG DE,
"FLY, HVAD FLYGTE KAN!
HVO STAR FOR DANMARKS KRISTIAN,
HVO STAR FOR DANMARKS KRISTIAN
I KAMP?"

(ENGLISH TRANSLATION)

KING CHRISTIAN STOOD BY THE LOFTY
MAST
IN MIST AND SMOKE;
HIS SWORD WAS HAMMERING SO FAST,
THROUGH GOTHIC HELM AND BRAIN IT
PASSED;
THEN SANK EACH HOSTILE HULK AND
MAST
IN MIST AND SMOKE.
"FLY!" SHOUTED THEY,
"FLY, HE WHO CAN!

NATIONAL ANTHEM OF DENMARK:
DER ER ET YNDIGT LAND

TO BE PLAYED WHEN DANISH ROYALTY IS NOT PRESENT.

(DANISH)

DER ER ET YNDIGT LAND,
DET STAR MED BREDE BOGE,
NAER SALTENOSTERSTRAND,
NAER SALTEN OSTERSTRAND.

DET BUGTER SIG I BAKKE, DAL,
DET HEDDER GAMLE DANMARK,
OG DET ER FREJAS SAL,
OG DET ER FREJAS SAL.

(ENGLISH TRANSLATION)

I KNOW A LOVELY LAND,
WHOSE CHARMING WOODS OF BEECHES
GROW NEAR THE BALTIC STRAND,
GROW NEAR THE BALTIC STRAND.

IT WAVES FROM VALLEY UP TO HILL,
IT'S NAME IS OLDEN DENMARK,
AND HERE DWELLS FREYA STILL,
AND HERE DWELLS FREYA STILL.

National Anthem of Denmark

To be played only when Danish Royalty is present.

Words by
Johannes Ewald (1743-1781)

Melody by
D.L. Rogert (1742-1848)

National Anthem of Denmark
To be played when Danish Royalty is not present.

Words by
Adam Gottlob Oehlenschlager (1779-1850)

Melody by
Hans Ernst Kroyer (1798-1879)

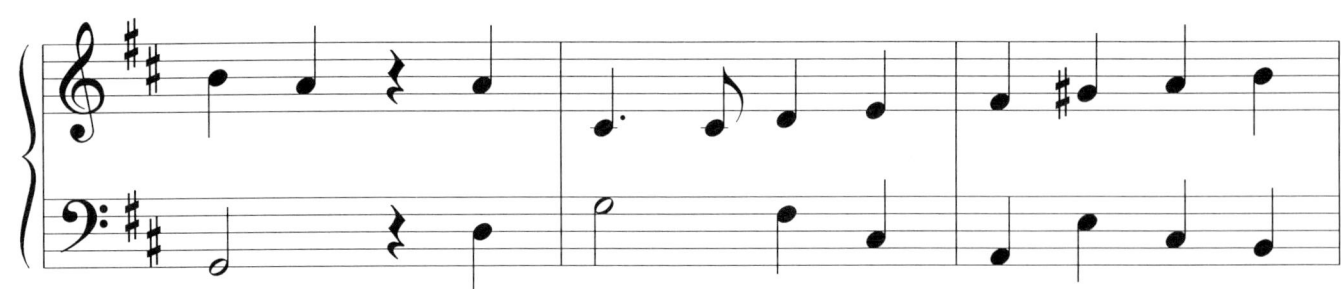

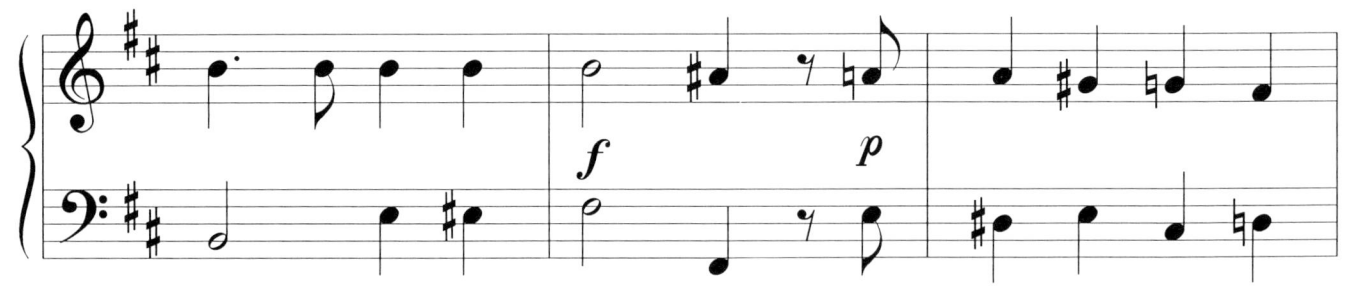

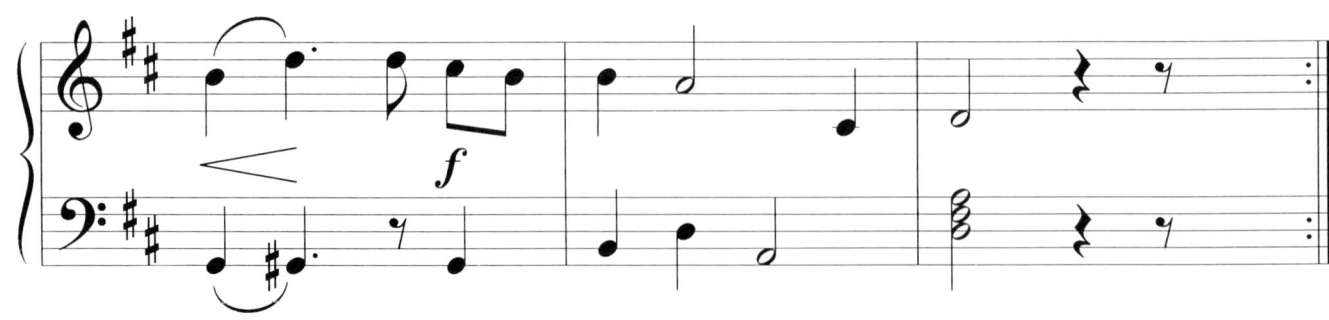

GERMANY

Form of Government: *Federal Republic*

Predominant Language: *German*

Capital: *Berlin*

Currency: *Mark*

National Holiday: *NA*

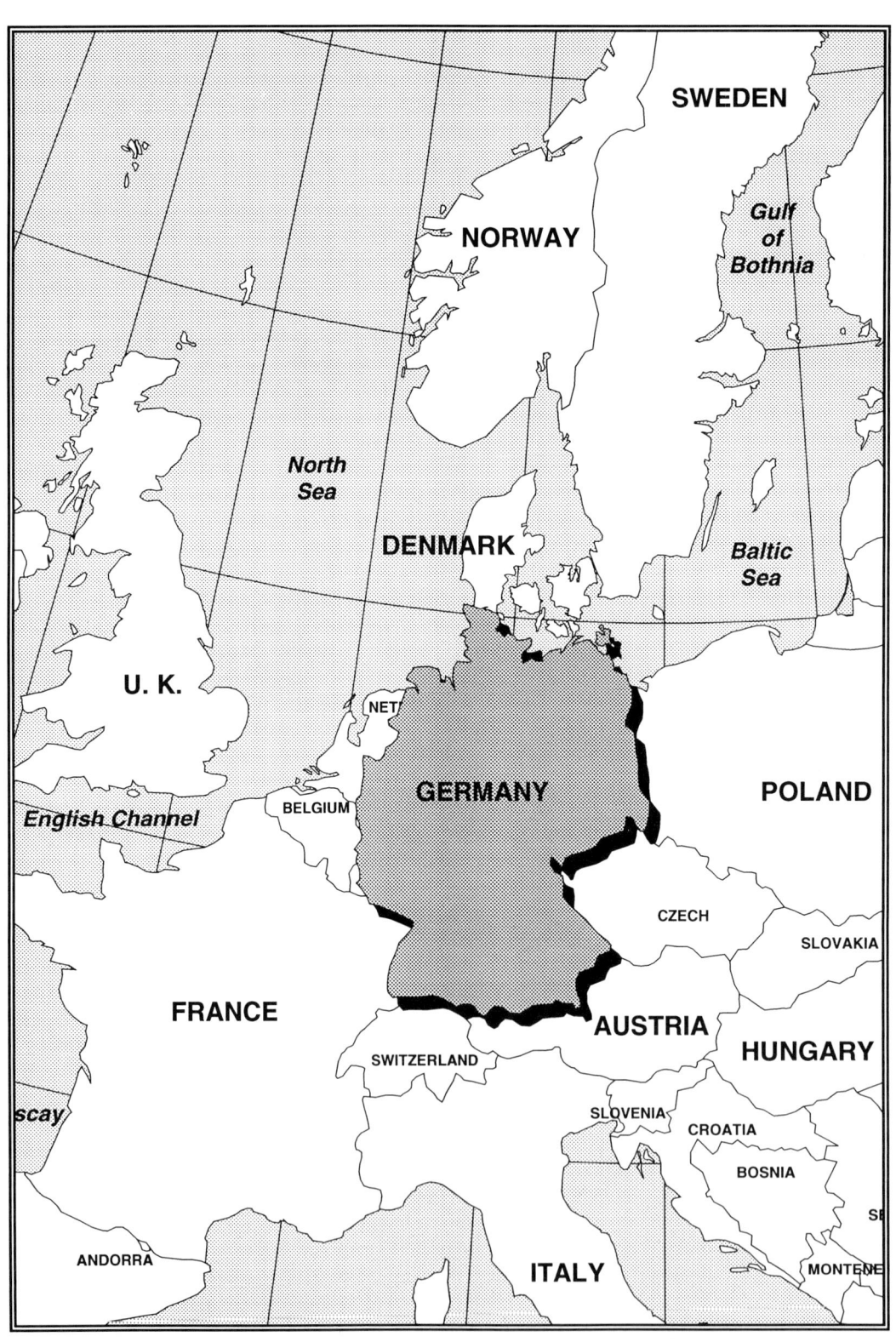

NATIONAL ANTHEM OF THE
FEDERAL REPUBLIC OF GERMANY:
DEUTSCHLAND-LIED

(GERMAN)

EINIGKEIT UND RECHT UND FREIHEIT
FUR DAS DEUTSCHE VATERLAND!
DANACH LASST UNS ALLE STREBEN
BRUDERLICH MIT HERZ UND HAND!
EINIGKEIT UND RECHT UND FREIHEIT
SIND DES GLUCKES UNTERPFAND
BLUH IM GLANZE DIESES GLUCKES
BLUHE DEUTSCHES VATERLAND!
BLUH IM GLANZE DIESES GLUCKES
BLUHE DEUTSCHES VATERLAND!

(ENGLISH TRANSLATION)

UNITY AND RIGHT AND FREEDOM
FOR THE GERMAN FATHERLAND;
LET US ALL WORK TO THIS GOAL
BROTHERLY, WITH HEARTS AND HANDS.
UNITY AND RIGHT AND FREEDOM
ARE THE PARTS OF HAPPINESS.
FLOURISH, IN THIS BLESSING'S GLORY
FLOURISH, GERMAN FATHERLAND.
FLOURISH IN THIS BLESSING'S GLORY
FLOURISH, GERMAN FATHERLAND.

National Anthem of Germany
Deutschland-Lied

Words by
Heinrich Hoffman Von Fallersleben (1798-1874)

Melody by
Franz Joseph Haydn (1732-1809)

LIECHTENSTEIN

Form of Government: *Constitutional Monarchy*

Predominant Language: *German*

Capital: *Vaduz*

Currency: *Swiss franc*

National Holiday: *St. Joseph's Day, March 19th*

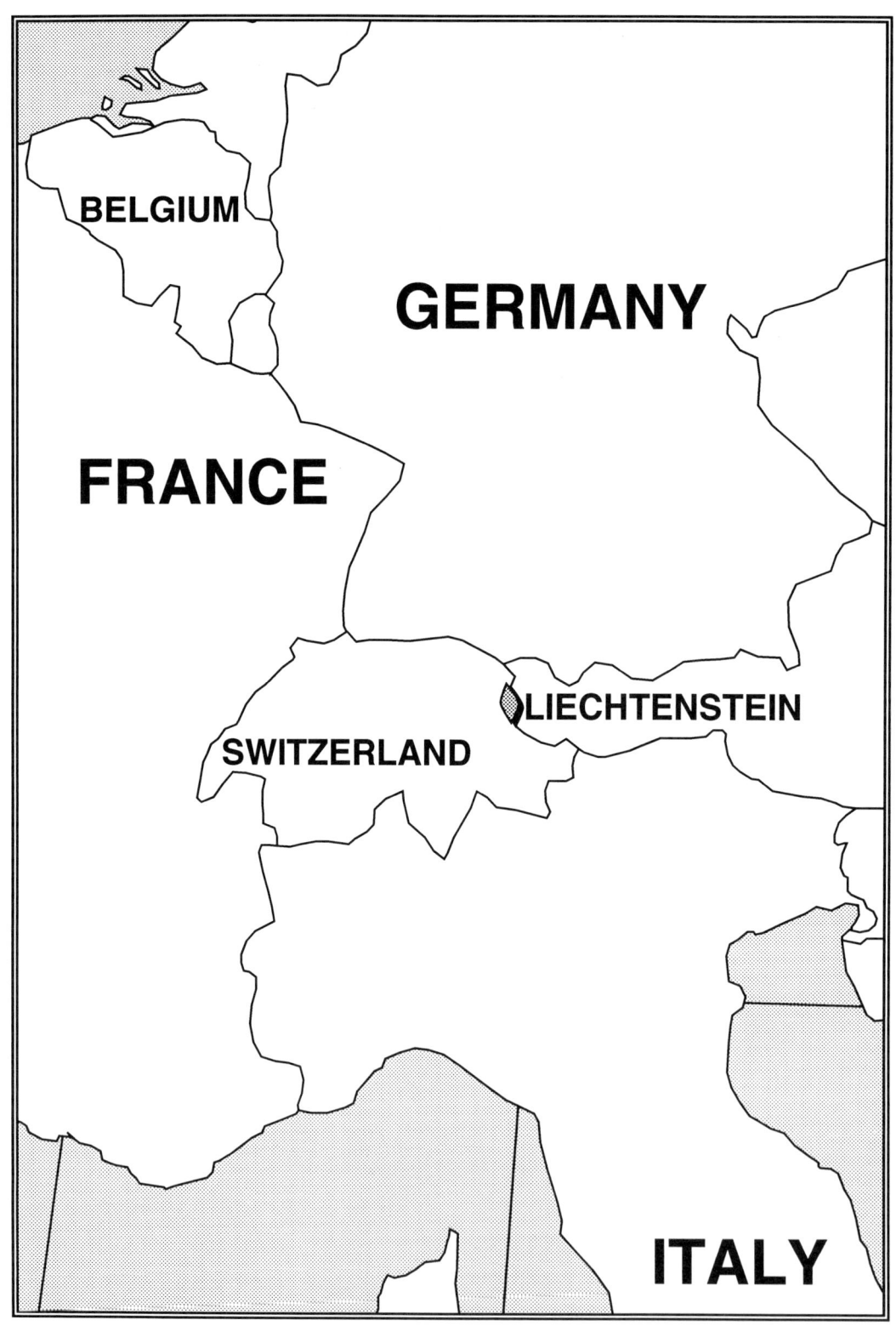

NATIONAL ANTHEM OF LIECHTENSTEIN:

(THE TUNE IS THE SAME AS GREAT BRITAIN.)

(GERMAN)

OBEN AM DEUTSCHEN RHEIN
LEHNET SICH LIECHTENSTEIN
AN ALPENHOH'N.
DIES LIEBE HEIMATLAND
IM DEUTSCHEN
VATERLAND HAT GOTTES WEISE HAND
FUR UNS ERSEH'N.

(ENGLISH TRANSLATION)

HIGH ABOVE THE GERMAN RHINE
LEANS LIECHTENSTEIN
AGAINST ALPINE SLOPES.
THIS BELOVED HOMELAND
IN THE GERMAN FATHERLAND
WAS CHOSEN FOR US BY
THE LORD'S WISDOM.

National Anthem of Liechtenstein

Words by
H.H. Jauch (1850)

Melody by
Unknown

LUXEMBOURG

Form of Government: *Constitutional Monarchy*

Predominant Languages: *Luxembourgian, French, German*

Capital: *Luxembourg*

Currency: *Lux Franc*

National Holiday: *National Day, June 23rd (Public celebration of the Grand Duke's birthday - 1921)*

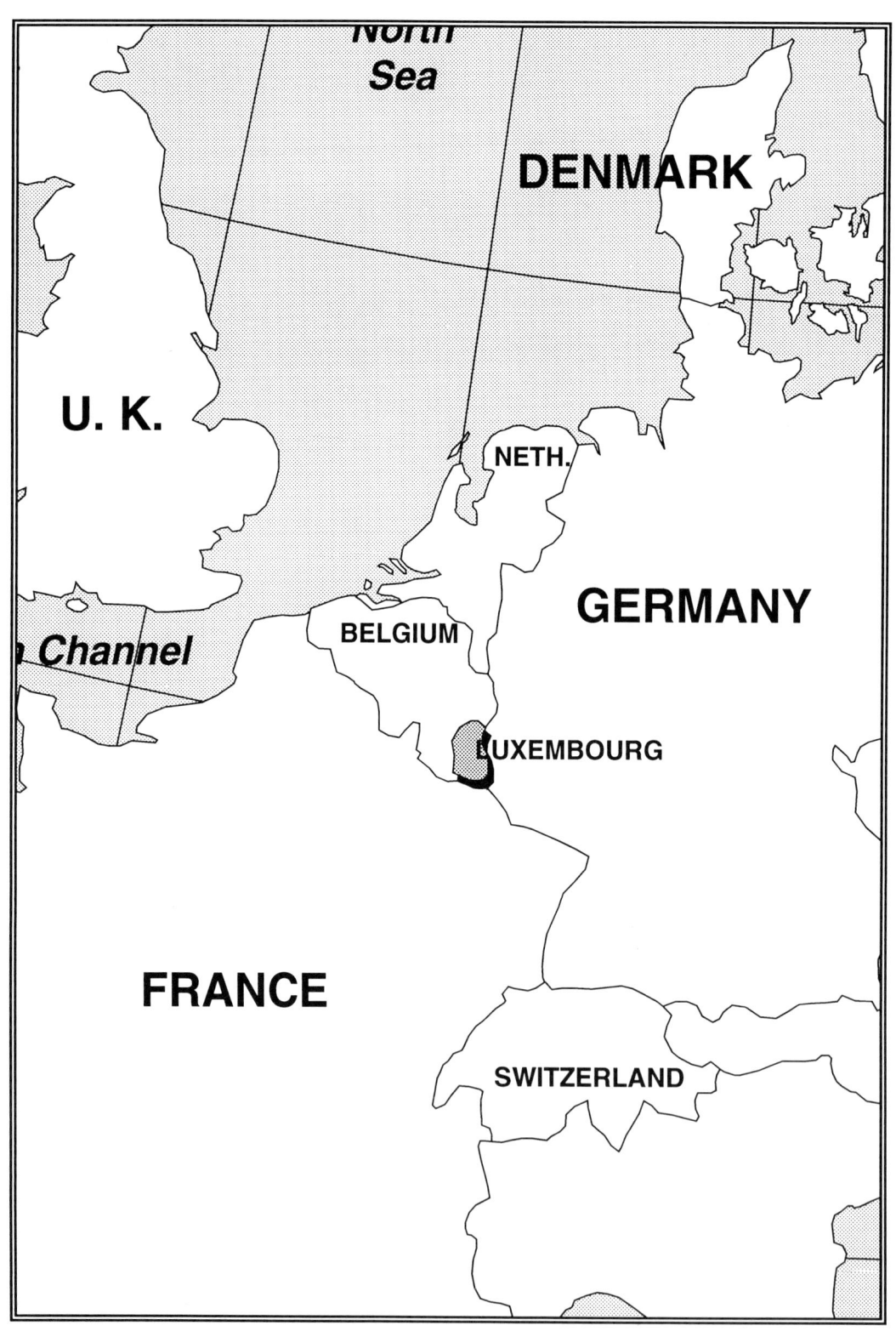

NATIONAL ANTHEM OF LUXEMBOURG:
INS HEMECHT

(LUXEMBOURG)

WO D'UOLZECHT DURECH D'WISEN ZET DURCH
D'FIELZEN D'SAUER BRECHT,
WO D'RIEF LAUSCHT D'MUSEL DOFTEG BLET,
DEN HIMMEL WEIN ONS MECHT;
DAT ASS ONS LAND FIR DAT MER
GEF HEINIDEN ALLES WO'N,
ONST HEMECHTSLAND DAT MIR
SO DEF AN ONSEN HIERZER DRO'N
ONST HEMECHTSLAND DAT MIR
SO DEF AN ONSEN HIERZER DRO'N!

(ENGLISH TRANSLATION)

WHERE SLOW YOU SEE THE ALZETTE FLOW,
THE SURA PLAY WILD PRANKS,
WHERE LOVELY VINEYARDS AMPLY GROW,
UPON THE MOSELLE'S BANKS,
THERE LIES THE LAND FOR WHICH OUR
THANKS
ARE OWED TO GOD ABOVE,
OUR OWN, OUR NATIVE LAND WHICH RANKS
WELL FOREMOST IN OUR LOVE.
OUR OWN, OUR NATIVE LAND WHICH RANKS
WELL FOREMOST IN OUR LOVE.

National Anthem of Luxembourg
Ons Hemecht - Our Motherland

Words by
Michael Lentz (1820-1893)

Melody by
J.A. Zinnen (1827-1898)

MONACO

Form of Government: *Constitutional Monarchy*

Predominant Languages: *French*

Capital: *Monaco*

Currency: *French franc*

National Holiday: *National Day, November 19th*

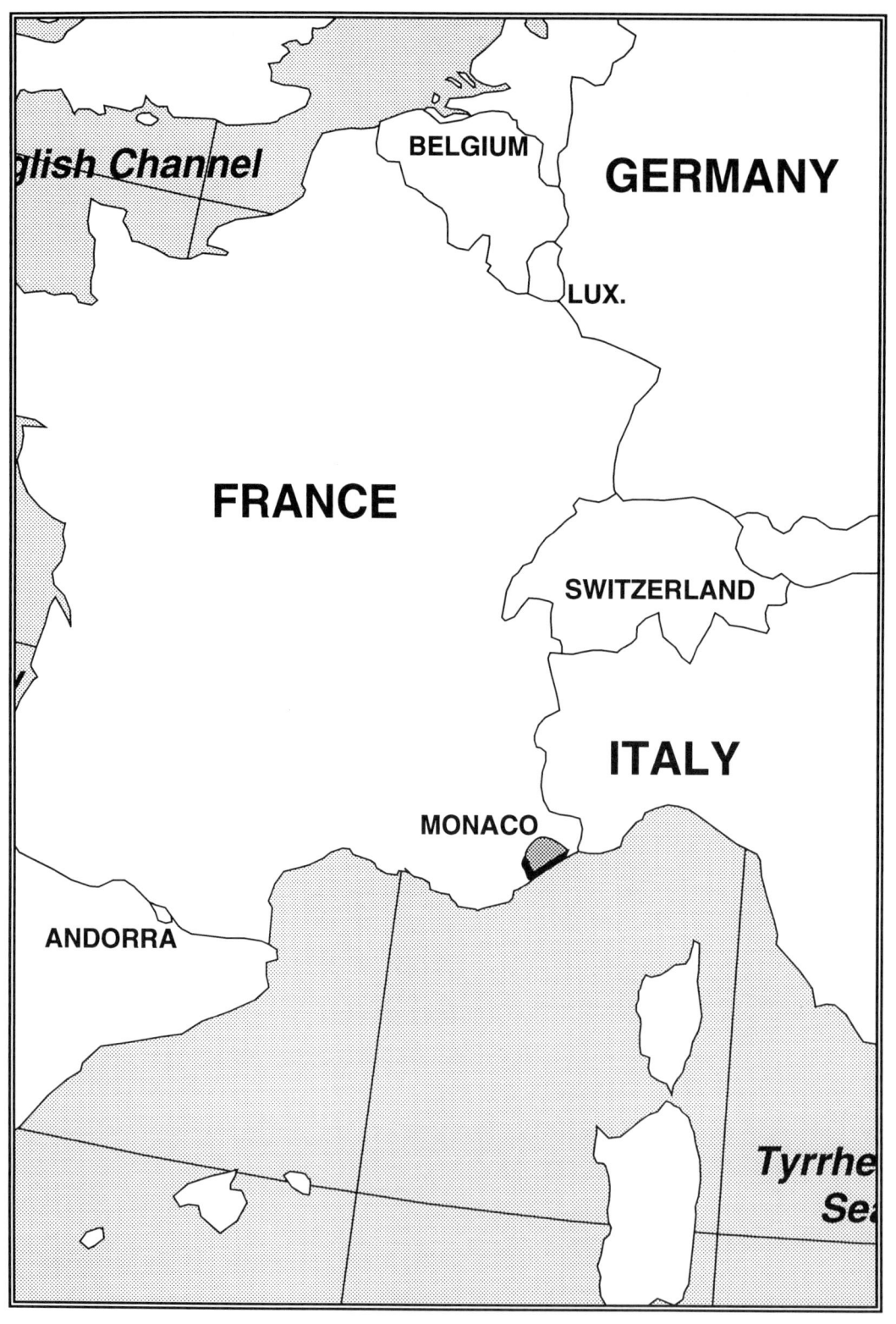

NATIONAL ANTHEM OF MONACO:

(FRENCH)

PRINCIPAUTE MONACO MA PATRIE,
OH! COMBIEN DIEU EST PRODIGUE POUR TOI.
CIEL TOUJOURS PUR,
RIVES TOUJOURS FLEURIES,
TON SOUVERAIN EST PLUS AIME QU'UN ROI.
TON SOUVERAIN EST PLUS AIME QU'UN ROI.

(ENGLISH TRANSLATION)

PRINCIPALITY OF MONACO, MY COUNTRY,
OH! HOW GOD IS LAVISH WITH YOU.
AN EVER-CLEAR SKY,
EVER-BLOSSOMING SHORES,
YOUR SOVEREIGN IS BETTER LIKED
THAN A KING.
YOUR SOVEREIGN IS BETTER LIKED
THAN A KING.

National Anthem of Monaco

Words by
Theophile Bellando De Castro (1820-1903)

Melody by
Albrecht (1817-1895)

Tempo di Marcia

NETHERLANDS

Form of Government: *Constitutional Monarchy*

Predominant Language: *Dutch*

Capital: *Amsterdam*

Currency: *Guilder*

National Holiday: *Queen's Day, April 30th (1938)*

NATIONAL ANTHEM OF NETHERLANDS: WILLIAM OF NASSAU

(DUTCH)

WILHELMUS VAN NASSOUWE
BANICK VAN DUITSCHEN BLOET;
DEN VADERLANT GHETROUWE BLIJFICK
TOT INDEN DOET.
EEN PRINCE VAN ORANJEN
BENICK VRIJ ONVERVEERT;
DEN CONINCK VAN HISPANJEN
HEBICK ALTIJD GHEEERT.

(ENGLISH TRANSLATION)

I, WILLIAM OF NASSAU,
DESCENDANT OF A DUTCH AND ANCIENT LINE,
I DEDICATE UNDYING FAITH
TO THIS LAND OF MINE.
A PRINCE I AM, UNDAUNTED,
OF ORANGE, EVER FREE.
TO THE KING OF SPAIN I'VE GRANTED
A LIFELONG LOYALTY.

National Anthem of Netherlands
Wilhelmus

Words by
Philip Marnix van St. Aldegonde (1540-1598)

Melody by
Unknown - prior to 1572

NORWAY

Form of Government: *Constitutional Monarchy*

Predominant Language: *Norwegian*

Capital: *Oslo*

Currency: *Krone*

National Holiday: *Constitution Day, May 17th (1814)*

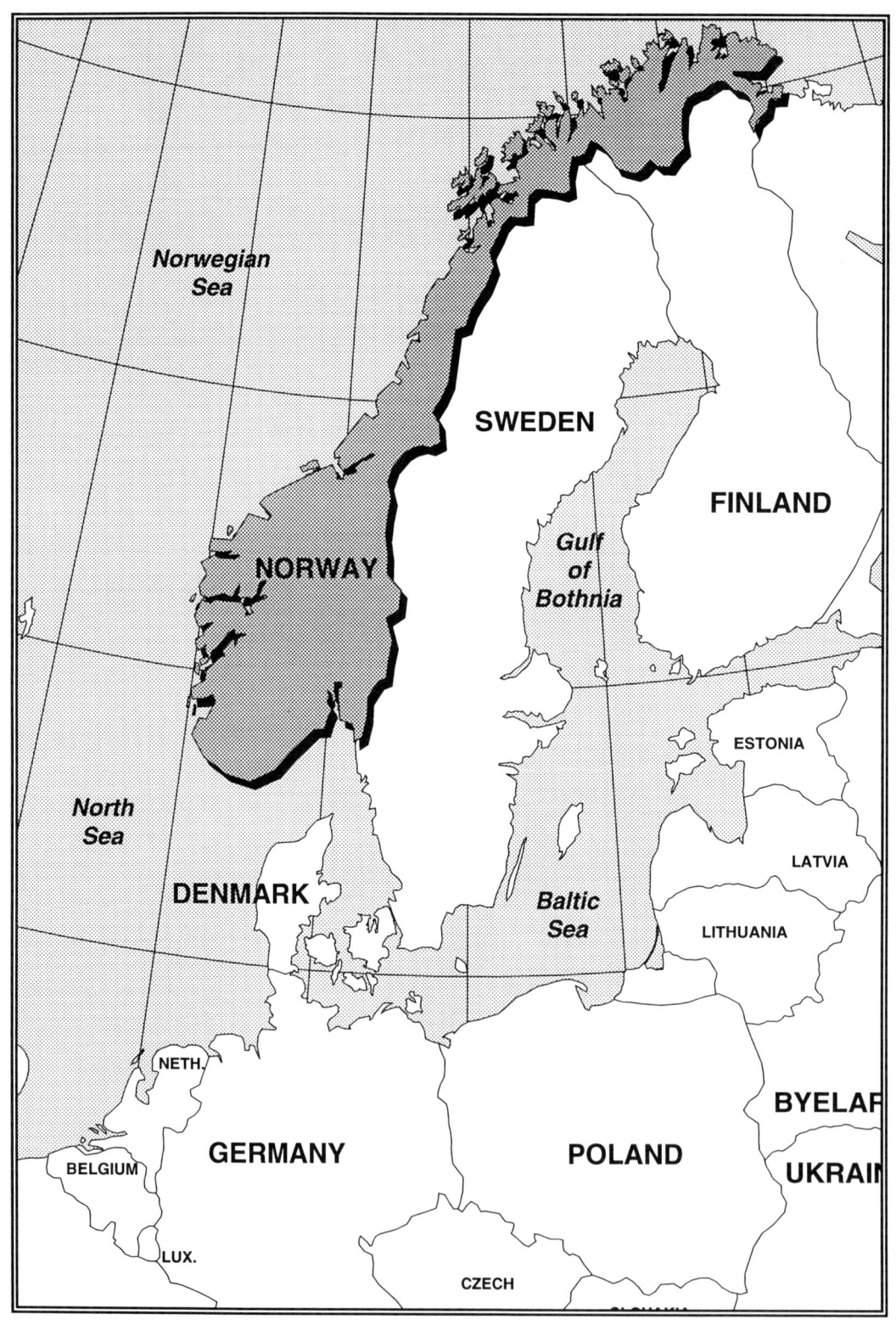

NATIONAL ANTHEM OF NORWAY:
JA, VI ELSKER DETTE LANDET

(NORWEGIAN)

JA, VI ELSKER DETTE LANDET,
SOM DET STIGER FREM,FURET,
VOERBITT OVER VANNET MED DE TUSEN HJEM.
ESLKER, ESLKERDET OG TENKER
PA VAR FAR OG MOR
OG DEN SAGANATT SOM SENKER
DROMME PA VAR JORD,
OG DEN SAGANATT SOM SENKER,
SENKER DROMME PA VAR JORD!

(ENGLISH TRANSLATION: GATHORNE-HARDY)

YES, WE LOVE WITH FOND DEVOTION THIS,
THE LAND THAT LOOMS RUGGED,
STORM-SCARRED, O'ER THE OCEANS,
WITH HER THOUSAND HOMES.
LOVE HER, IN OUR LOVE RECALLING
THOSE WHO GAVE US BIRTH,
AND OLD TALES WHICH NIGHT, IN FALLING,
BRINGS AS DREAMS, AS DREAMS TO EARTH.

National Anthem of Norway
Ja, vi elsker dette landet

Words by
Bjornsterne Bjornsson (1832-1910)

Melody by
Rikard Nordraak (1842-1866)

SWITZERLAND

Form of Government: *Federal Republic*

Predominant Languages: *German, French, Italian, Romansh*

Capital: *Bern*

Currency: *Swiss Franc*

National Holiday: *Anniversary of the founding of the Swiss Confederation, August 1st (1291)*

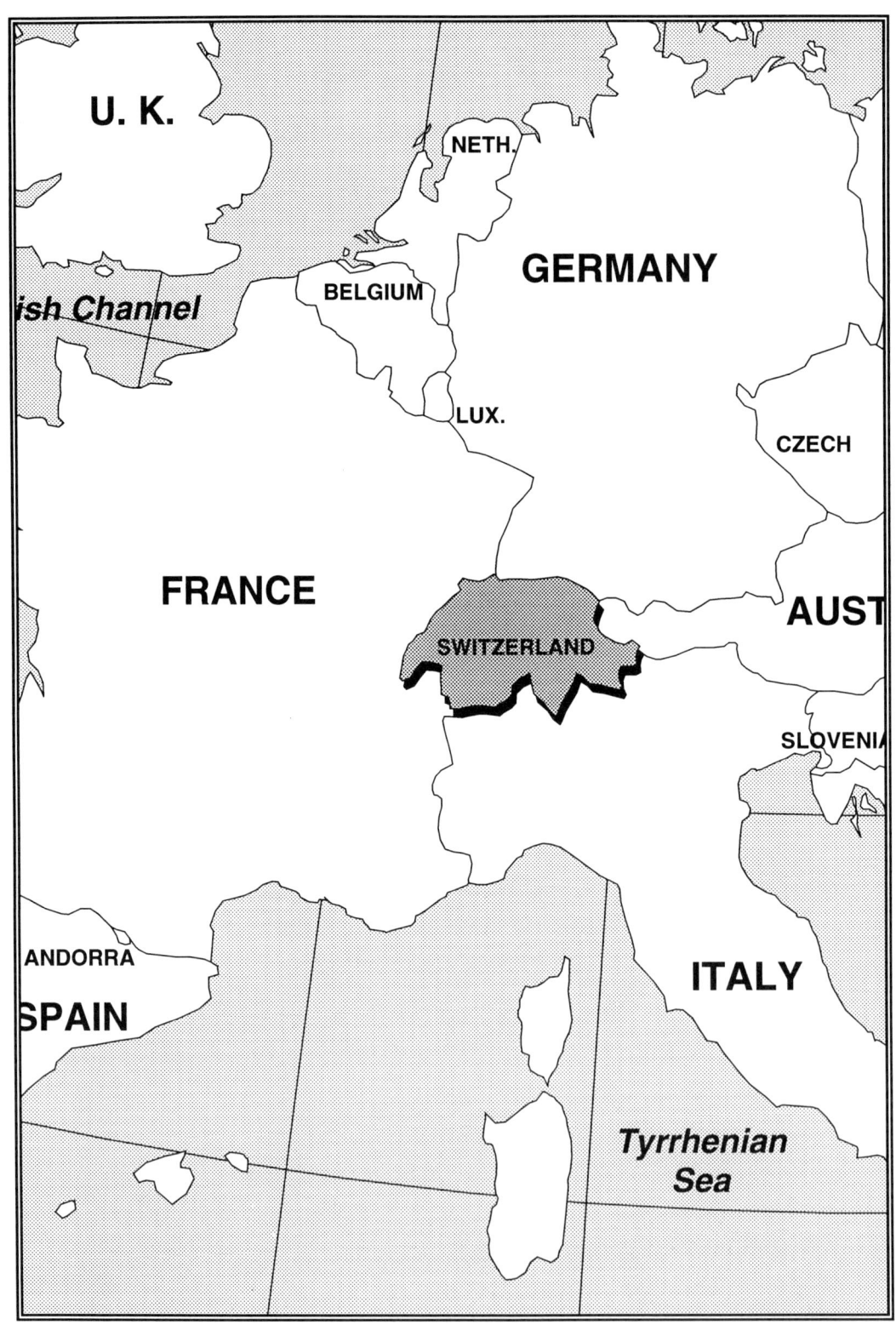

NATIONAL ANTHEM OF SWITZERLAND: SWISS SPALM

(GERMAN)

TRITTST IM MORGENROT DEHER,
SEH ICH DICH IM STRAHLENMEER,
DICH, DU HOCHERHABENER,HERRLICHER!
WENN DER ALPENFIRN SICH ROTET,
BETET, FREIE SCHWEIZER, BETET!
EURE FROMME SEELE AHNT,
EURE FROMME SEELE AHNT,
GOTT IM HEHREN VATERLAND,
GOTT IM HEHREN VATERLAND!

(ENGLISH TRANSLATION)

WHEN THE MORNING SKIES GROW RED
AND O'ER US THEIR RADIANCE SHED,
THOU, O LORD, APPEARETH IN THEIR LIGHT.
WHEN THE ALPS GLOW BRIGHT
WITH SPLENDOR,
PRAY TO GOD, TO HIM SURRENDER,
FOR YOU FEEL AND UNDERSTAND,
FOR YOU FEEL AND UNDERSTAND
THAT HE DWELLETH IN THIS LAND,
THAT HE DWELLETH IN THIS LAND.

National Anthem of Switzerland
Schweizerpsalm - Swiss Psalm

Words by
Leonhard Widmer (1808-1867)

Melody by
P. Alberich Zwyssig (1808-1854)